A **Cup**
of *Poetry*

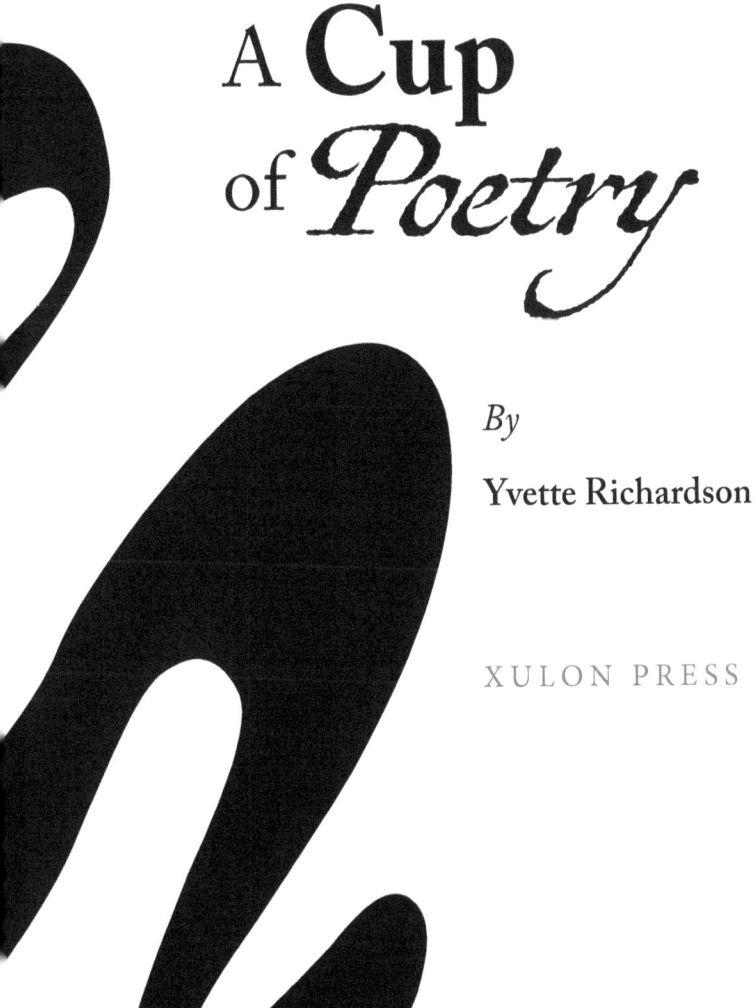

A Cup of Poetry

By

Yvette Richardson

XULON PRESS

Xulon Press
2301 Lucien Way #415
Maitland, FL 32751
407.339.4217
www.xulonpress.com

© 2021 by Yvette Richardson

All rights reserved solely by the author. The author guarantees all contents are original and do not infringe upon the legal rights of any other person or work. No part of this book may be reproduced in any form without the permission of the author. The views expressed in this book are not necessarily those of the publisher.

Due to the changing nature of the Internet, if there are any web addresses, links, or URLs included in this manuscript, these may have been altered and may no longer be accessible. The views and opinions shared in this book belong solely to the author and do not necessarily reflect those of the publisher. The publisher therefore disclaims responsibility for the views or opinions expressed within the work.

Unless otherwise indicated, Scripture quotations taken from the King James Version (KJV)–*public domain*.

Paperback ISBN-13: 978-1-6628-3406-6
eBook ISBN-13: 978-1-6628-3407-3

Table of Contents

Letting Go 1
Breathe 2
Changes 3
Seasons 4
Decisions 5
Life is God 6
Engaged 7
Good Fruit 8
Motivation 9
Seasons of Work............................ 10
Trapped 11
Demoted 12
Baby 13
Gone Too Soon............................. 14
Joy 15
Morning 16
Listen 17
Visits 18
Loss 19
Valley Moments and Mountain Tops................ 20
Woman of Faith 21
The Good Girls 23
Family 24
Sisterhood 25
G-BABY IS HERE 26

Letting Go

I'm letting go of past hurts, pains, and sorrows they are buried now,

I'm letting go of the now that press me with issues, complaints, and confusion they are resting now,

I'm letting go of what could have been, going to be, and already is and listening to the winds that says;

I am here but I'm in control. Letting go today will give me peace, joy and love for myself, myself, and myself.

Written after being hospitalized 2/12/09 (Entered in a contest with Eber & Wein Publishing Company 12/31/10-made it as a semi-finalist. {Published}

Breathe

Breathe in, breathe out

What's that smell?

I feel as if I can tell

Breathe in, breathe out

The calmness of a new rising

And the beginning of freedom

As the ocean flows the tide rise

We see the sun glistening over it…

What a breath of fresh air and the amazing God who gave us the breath of life.

Breathe!

Written after being hospitalized and not able to rest 2/13/09

Changes

Life throws us curves that we don't quite understand

But with God you won't fall into quicksand.

It's the changes in life that seems to make us determined to stand

because God has an ultimate plan.

If you live by the changes that God has set, than you will know that His path will never let you down.

So with this in mind remember Romans 8:28 and know that God is never late.

Continue to walk in your Call and your Purpose!

Dedicated to Daughter Amber Vonee' Richardson on the day we left her for college. 8/11/09

Seasons

Move with the clouds in unity as seasons change to help the community of faith,

Fall branches out leaves to equip us with the preserves that God allowed to help us stand

Winter keeps the heart warm so that the Agape love given by God will be expressed constantly through his people

Spring blossoms the uniqueness of God's colors of life to keep breathing, feeling and seeing so that people can continue to feel his presence

The summer flowed with God's entire children active in family gatherings. It showers down the blessings of the continuous generations of seeds that He put on this earth.

The seasons are a good solid foundation to remind us of the awesomeness of God.

Written 8/16/10 and 9/4/10

Decisions

We make decisions each and every day but how many times have we seen our visions come to play.

Seeking to make our own dreams come true

We visualized, write and sing sometimes until we are blue.

This doesn't mean we fall in desperation of giving up

It just means we decide to do, so we won't be stuck in procrastination.

Make a decision and make it right because it effects the rest of your life.

Written 8/12/10

Life is God

Life is the heart beat within the womb

It carries its only love song until it burst out on the tomb.

When life arrives it has instructions ordained by God himself.

The parents take life, hold it with so much pride, but know that the instructions given are done in stride.

One key way of staying faithful is remembering life is God, breathe and trusting Him will set you free.

Moving in a new home in Covington-transition for Amber 2006
Starting a new school, new change, new friends and a new county

Engaged

A diamond, two or three a proposal box in my hand on bended knee.

Where do I go, where should I take her;

Should it be unique or should it be a place she is familiar with.

Oh my, how excited I am tonight to see the look on my future daughter-in-law face to be.

"Taylor"

9/24/10

Good Fruit

Grounded in good soil, planted and watered

Branched off from generation to generation to sow seeds of good fruit

Fruits of love, joy, peace, patience, kindness, goodness, faithfulness, gentleness and self-control

These fruits are the foundation of our lives and of the spirit

Inspired word of Scripture 10/11/10

Motivation

Urge, push, nudge, encouragement are all a part of motivation.

I need the water, a walk, to listen, a calmness, an assurance, the voice of wisdom and that great cloud of witnesses along with a true friend who says,

YOU CAN DO IT!!!

MOTIVATION

10/11/10

Seasons of Work

Spring, Summer, Winter, Fall somehow we work them all.

Never understanding how good we are because sometimes the distance is spread afar.

We work, work, and work until it seems as if the days run into months not really knowing if appreciated or denunciated.

How can one determine their worth in the seasons of work?

Only our Master knows, only our Master knows the seasons of our work.

10/11/10

Trapped

Dipping and hiding going hard for something but not the treasure.

You searched wondering when the opportunity will arise but time pass and you realized options are gone.

You look up and there you are, trapped.

10/11/10

Demoted

Emotional, angry, free, confused, tired, upset, going backwards and relief are all the feelings within.

God always knows best even if we don't but what now.

Keep moving, going, staying, ministering, and remembering the purpose.

Did you forget, set aside or get stressed out because of strong holds?

Demoted sometimes a blessing in disguise, people really not knowing the full intention of what surmised.

God is a mystery but in His timing all will be revealed.

All clear to be refreshed and renewed.

10/11/10

Baby

Baby on its way

Any day now

Yes, we will have to pray

Mom is a little anxious

Since it's been a while she's been in this way

No matter what, we are expecting a great big celebrating day.

Twiddle Dee, Twiddle Dum

There is nothing more yum yum

than a baby in his mother's loving arms

Little baby, little baby,

We are going to sound off a Great Alarm!

Inspired by my sister Felicia's pregnancy with Elianna 11/2/10

Gone Too Soon

Gone too soon but not forgotten

Memories shared in our minds forever

Stories told will be shared as lessons

Laughter on our faces will remind us of the treasure

That you were gone too soon

Dedicated to Grandma Lillie Pearl Swearinger 11/11/10

Joy

It is unspeakable, laughable, uncontrollable, excitable, exuberant or just overjoyed;

unexplainable pure joy!

How I was feeling 11/11/10

Morning

It's a new dawning

The sun just peeks above the sky

Just a little bit to say its morning

It called out to the heavens to clear the darkness out and just as it did

The heavens responded with the full morning light

A good day/morning 11/11/10

Listen

Listen to me

I have a voice

Listen to me

I have concerns

Listen to me

I have issues

Do you care? Are you listening?

So many things misunderstood.

Listen

After having an appointment with pain doctor 11/10/10

Visits

Picnics, movies, and eats

Relaxation, shopping and treats

Talking, reminiscing and playing.

Visits are so unique.

Play date with Auntie Juanita and Grandma Mildred 11/11/10

Loss

It can be detrimental to us here on earth because of the bond we share with the ones we love but the greatest thing I've learned is that God is love.

If our love ones and even ourselves have accepted Christ we have an even greater bond and that's the love of Jesus. We can celebrate the loss because we shall meet again in that great getting up morning, fair ye well…we shall meet again.

After losing some love ones 2/18/13

Valley Moments and Mountain Tops

Our life experience teaches us about valley moments and mountain tops.

How we get there is through our rough spots and cloudy days.

The hurl of the winds came and we twirl right on through it.

The spins and floods push us to we bend and break but as friends and brethren we rose together to rebuild.

The mountain seems steep but we begin to climb, because we know we will reap, when we reach the top.

Now step by step we climb being careful of our footing while making sure we're steady as the belt is wrapped around us to guide.

To the top we climb, to the top we climb, this is how we survive.

From our valley moments to our mountain tops.

Woman of Faith

She stands with power that God has given her even if she is alone.

She ignites the power within others by her example.

She inspires you by her faith in God.

Motivates you to move in spite of, because of, and who God is.

The ignition of His power grows even stronger within as she enlightens the path of those who knows her and those who don't.

The unfeigned faith is one who stands the test of time-this is where she is purge through the fire and become a beautiful precious jewel.

A woman of faith prays for others. She intercedes, touch and agree, believe by faith that God will deliver and answer their prayers.

She walks believing and knowing that the promises that God has spoken to her will be done. Her healing, finances in the overflow, vision will come to pass. She has seen it and she knows that whatever God has spoken it shall be.

A woman of faith doesn't waiver. She rest in the arms of God. She knows where her strength comes from.

She is dependent on God alone because there is no failure in God.

She prays first, listens and responds.

The communion with God is what a Woman of Faith exemplifies.

In honor of my First Lady, Minister Antoinette Carson

1/27/2013

The Good Girls

One you would think that is pure, clean, and discreet

But the taunts are one that is not so unique.

We hold our heads high with respect to what our name proclaim

To find out it's only a way to show disdain

Not from us but from those ignorant to understand it's not a game

So with that in mind

The Good Girls put them to shame.

1/15/11

Family

They are not perfect but they are knit together through blood and generations.

We come in different colors, shapes, sizes, and places but we are destined to be together in this nation.

We are here to love, cherish, and help one another but most importantly to free each other to be individuals as Family.

11/22/11-2/20/12

Sisterhood

Girlfriends, cousins, and sisters alike how much in common are we too bright.

We sit eat, muddle, talk and share; knowing good and well we are fully aware that our challenges and circumstances are only a test so that when it's over we have done our best.

Encourage, Nurture and worship are our best part of giving to help us foster our corporate living.

Allowing us to be a part of Sisterhood will continue to be therapeutic, energetic, and unified within.

Sisterhood is linked from our hearts to our lives forever.

Dedicated to "the Girls" my traveling Sisters 9/12/12

G-Baby Is Here

As we looked through the window they held you up

We stared in amazement how beautiful you are

So tiny, so small, with a full head of hair

You had the prettiest brown skinned and freckled cheeks to match

We never thought our heart could contain so much love until you appeared on the scene

Remarkable, Wonderful, and Miracle you are

Thank you Zaia Nechelle for allowing us to be your MeMa' and PaPa'.

August 27, 2013 (Born July 10, 2013)

www.ingramcontent.com/pod-product-compliance
Ingram Content Group UK Ltd.
Pitfield, Milton Keynes, MK11 3LW, UK
UKHW041948230426
12048UKWH00008B/203